JAZZING IT UP

How To Improvise with Jazz Chords On Guitar

by Fred Sokolow

Edited by Ronny S. Schiff
Graphic Design by Elyse Wyman
Cover photo by E.K. Waller

Schiff/Sokolow Publishing

Copyright © 2001 Schiff/Sokolow Publishing
Los Angeles, California

members.aol.com/sokolowmus/

contents

introduction

One of the main things that distinguishes jazz from other types of music is the jazz musician's use of *chords*. Instead of being limited by a chord progression, the jazz player uses a given set of chords as a springboard for improvisation. By some jazz alchemy, Joe Pass or Chick Corea makes a standard twelve bar blues sound contemporary and innovative; Bill Evans changes the theme song from Walt Disney's "Alice In Wonderland" into a modern jazz waltz.

Jazz players transform pop, blues or even folk tunes into jazz by changing the music's chord structure, adding, embellishing and bending it to suit their personal style. The knowledge it takes to do this — a large repertoire of chords, an understanding of how progressions work, and a sense of how and when to substitute one chord for another — is part of the ABCs of jazz. You need these skills to play jazz.

The purpose of this book isn't to increase your repertoire with jazz versions of "Dixie" and other folk songs. The idea is *to demonstrate, with simple tunes that everyone knows, how you can improvise with chords like a jazz player does.* Starting with a chord dictionary and a study of chord groups, you'll learn many substitution ideas and theories of chord movement. This preliminary work will prepare you for a series of jazz versions of simple, familiar songs, plus detailed analyses of how each tune was given a jazz sound. There's also a section on creative comping (chord back-up).

Hopefully, after digesting this material you'll know how to re-shape a tune to *your* liking in a jazz vein... and you'll have a better understanding of chord progressions and chord improvisation.

CHORD GROUPS

To help you organize your thinking about jazz chords, they are grouped in the following pages into five categories, according to the intervals* they contain: major, minor, dominant seventh, augmented and diminished.

The chord grids listed in each category are identified by *type*, such as Major 7th or Minor 9th. No letter names (G, C♯) are given. *The root note of each chord is circled,* so you can make any formation correspond to a desired letter (e. g. make a Major 7th formation into G Maj7) by matching its root note to the appropriate fret. For example:

Maj7

This chord ▦ is Gmaj7 when moved up to the 5th fret, because the (root) 4th string/5th fret is "G."

Practice moving each formation around the fretboard and naming it by its root note.*

Some of the chords below are *inversions* (chords whose lowest note is not their root). For example, MAJOR/3RD BASS means: a major chord with the third in the bass. (This is abbreviated to read M/3.)

Study the chord formations listed in each category and become familiar with them. Use any left-hand fingering you find comfortable. Notice that many of the chords are nearly identical. For instance, the first eight major chord formations are all the same as the first chord, minus one or two notes.

MAJOR CHORDS

The intervals 1, 3, and 5 make a major chord. Adding other intervals creates variations, as the chart below illustrates:

$$MAJOR = 1, 3, 5$$
$$SIXTH = 1, 3, 5, 6$$
$$MAJOR SEVENTH = 1, 3, 5, 7$$
$$MAJOR NINTH = 1, 3, 5, 7, 9$$

$$ADD NINE = 1, 3, 5, 9$$
$$SIX-NINE = 1, 3, 5, 6, 9$$
$$SUSPENDED = 1, 4, 5$$
$$SIX-NINE FLAT FIVE = 1, 3, ♭5, 6, 9$$

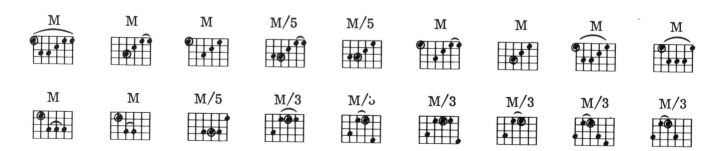

*See the MUSIC THEORY APPENDIX for futher explanation.

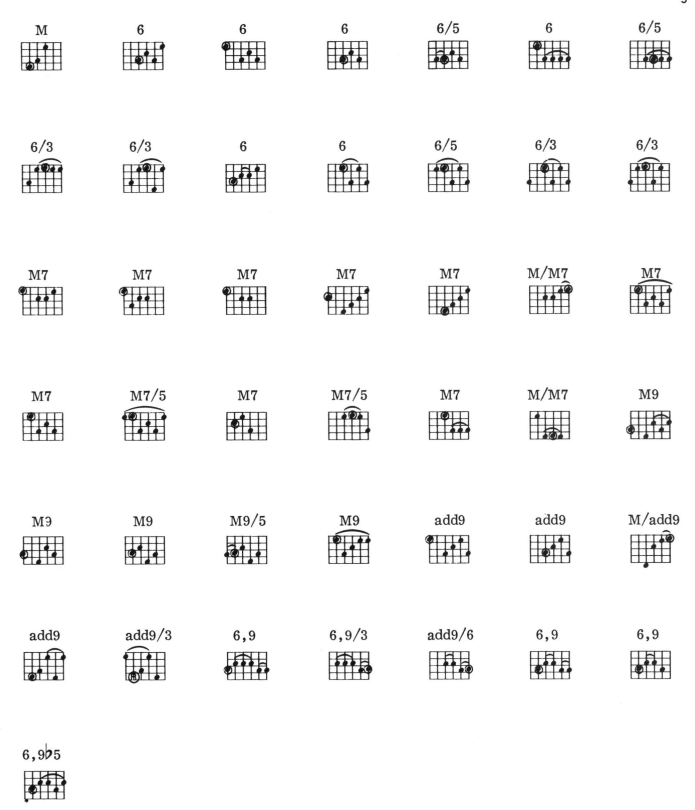

Careful analysis of these chords will reveal that some chord forms omit certain intervals. For example, some MAJOR NINE chords omit the third or fifth. When the *root* is omitted, an "R" appears, as a reference point, where root *could* be played.

The list of chords above, and the lists that follow, include all the chord forms used in the twelve tunes in this book. There are thousands more possible chord forms. One of the peculiarities of jazz guitar playing is that no two guitarists use the same exact repertory of chords.

MINOR CHORDS

The intervals 1, ♭3 and 5 make a minor chord. Sometimes the flatted third is called a minor third (written m3rd).

The varieties of minor chords include:

MINOR = 1, ♭3, 5

MINOR SEVENTH = 1, ♭3, 5, ♭7

MINOR SIXTH   = 1, ♭3, 5, 6

MINOR NINTH   = 1, ♭3, 5, ♭7, 9

MINOR SIX–NINE = 1, ♭3, 5, 6, 9

MINOR SEVEN FLAT FIVE = 1, ♭3, ♭5, ♭7

(sometimes called a half-diminished chord, written: ø)

MINOR ELEVEN = 1, ♭3, 5, ♭7, 11

MINOR ELEVEN FLAT FIVE = 1, ♭3, ♭5, ♭7, 11

MINOR, MAJOR SEVEN = 1, ♭3, 5, 7

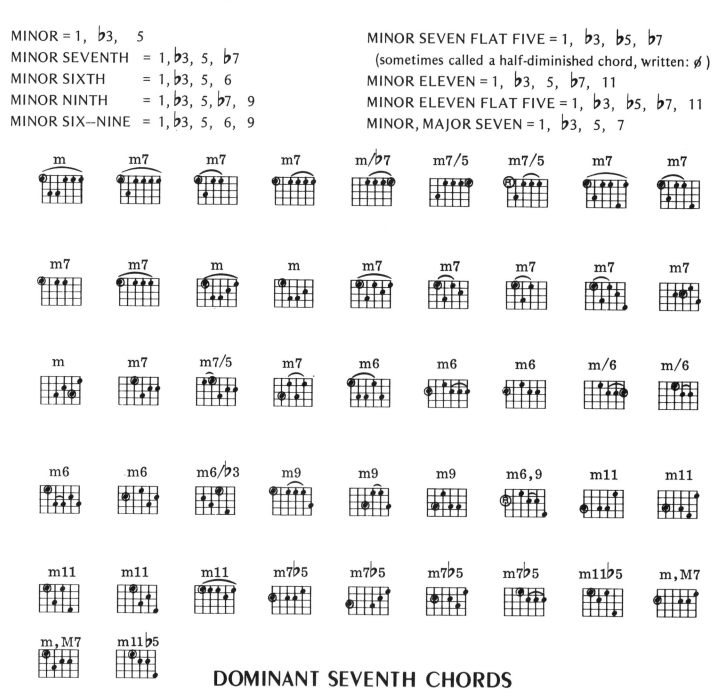

DOMINANT SEVENTH CHORDS

1, 3, 5, and ♭7 make a dominant seventh chord.

Within the dominant seventh group is a "sub-family" of suspended chords — chords that include a 4th. The eleventh chords are in this sub-family, because (except for the added 9th) they are identical to 7th/sus chords. The 11th is the same note as the 4th, an octave higher.

Sometimes 11th chords are written as fractions; e.g. D11 is written C/D. A C triad with D in the bass is the same as D11 because the C chord's 1, 3 and 5 are the D chord's ♭7, 9 and 11. In the listings below, chords of this type are written M/2 (a major chord with the 2nd in the bass). Chords like M7/2 (e.g. CM7/D) and m9/4 (Am9/D) are extensions of this type of 11th chord, as an examination of their intervals will reveal.

As you study these chord lists, you may notice that some chord forms have two or three names, depending on which note is considered the root. For instance, this fingering is a m7♭5 chord:

The same form, with a 1st string root, is a m6 chord. With an "unplayed root" on the 6th string/1st fret, it's a 7th ♭9 augmented chord.

Varieties of DOMINANT SEVENTH CHORDS include:

SEVENTH = 1, 3, 5, ♭7
SEVENTH FLAT FIVE = 1, 3, ♭5, ♭7
SEVENTH AUGMENTED (7+) = 1, 3, ♯5, ♭7
SEVENTH SUSPENDED = 1, 4, 5, ♭7
SEVEN FLAT NINE = 1, 3, 5, ♭7, ♭9
SEVEN SHARP NINE = 1, 3, 5, ♭7, ♯9
SEVEN FLAT NINE AUGMENTED = 1, 3, ♯5, ♭7, ♭9
SEVEN SHARP NINE AUGMENTED = 1, 3, ♯5, ♭7, ♯9

NINTH = 1, 3, 5, ♭7, 9
NINTH AUGMENTED = 1, 3, ♯5, ♭7, 9
NINE FLAT FIVE = 1, 3, ♭5, ♭7, 9
ELEVENTH = 1, 3, 5, ♭7, 9, 11
ELEVENTH AUGMENTED = 1, 3, 5, ˙7, 9, ♯11
THIRTEENTH = 1, 3, 5, ♭7, 9, 13
THIRTEEN FLAT NINE = 1, 3, 5, ♭7, ♭9, 13

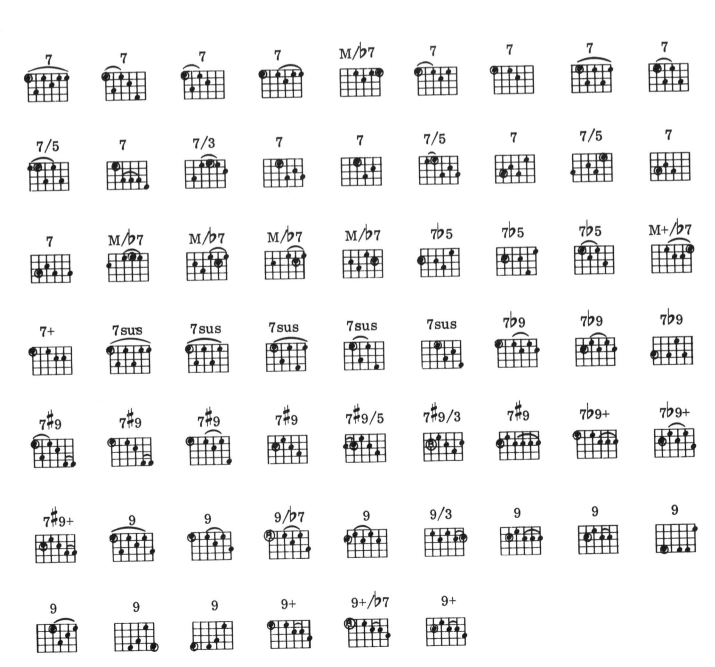

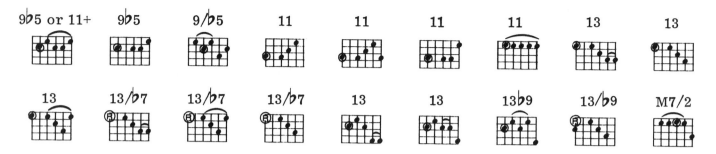

DIMINISHED CHORDS

Diminished chords are dominant sevenths in which everything is flatted but the root. The diminished chord is: 1, $\flat 3$, $\flat 5$, $\flat\flat 7$ ($\flat\flat 7 = 6$).

Ascending minor thirds make a diminished chord. If you climb by minor thirds on the guitar, you'll notice that after the fourth step you begin to repeat yourself (the 5th note in your climb is an octave above the 1st). Since you could start at any of the four steps in your ascent and arrive at the same four-note chord, each diminished chord has four names; that is, any of the four notes of a diminished chord can be considered the root. For example, C° can also be called E$\flat$°, G$\flat$° or A°, because all four chords are made of C, E$\flat$, G$\flat$ and A.

Because the diminished chord is made of ascending minor thirds, each time you move the *whole chord form* up a minor third (3 frets) you get a different voicing of the same chord.

Here are some diminished chord forms:

AUGMENTED CHORDS

The augmented chord is: 1, 3, $\sharp 5$. Ascending thirds make an augmented chord. After three ascending thirds you start to repeat yourself an octave higher; so, like a diminished chord, any note of the augmented chord can be considered its root, depending on the context within a chord progression. C+, E+ and G$\sharp$+ all are made of C, E, and G$\sharp$. Move an augmented chord up by thirds (four frets) and you get more voicings of the same chord.

Here are some augmented chord forms:

SUBSTITUTION IDEAS

The substitution ideas listed here are the methods a jazz soloist uses to alter and vary chords and chord progressions. You'll find several examples of each idea in the chord solos that follow. As you study each "rule" of substitution, try to apply it to a few tunes with which you're already familiar.

The bottom-line rule in substitution is to play whatever sounds good to you. Let your ear tell you which, if any, of these ideas is appropriate at any given moment.

DIRECT SUBSTITUTION

For any given chord, substitute another chord of the same letter-name in the same chord group. For instance instead of C, play C6 or CM7. You may choose a particular substitute because of the melody note the song calls for at that moment (the melody note may be a 6th or ♭5th), or because of an appropriate "tone coloration."

Chord types have tonal qualities which affect your substitution choices. Suspended chords and elevenths sound unresolved and suspenseful, while major chords, sixths and six-nine chords are more "at rest." Minor six-nine chords hold more tension than minor sevenths. Dominant-seven-sharp-nine chords sound dissonant where major sevens and major nines are "pretty" . . .and so on. As you become familiar with jazz chords (by playing them a lot), you'll form your own impressions of their tonal qualities.

PASSING CHORDS

"Inbetween chords" that help you get from one chord to another are called *passing chords*. The many ways to choose passing chords are discussed under the headings: FLAT FIFTH SUBSTITUTION, SCALEWISE SUBSTITUTION, DOMINANT MINOR SUBSTITUTION, APPROACH CHORDS, and BASS-LINE-DIRECTED SUBSTITUTION.

RELATIVE MINOR AND MAJOR SUBSTITUTION

For any major chord, substitute its relative minor. The relative minor chord is a m3rd below its relative major (e.g. Am is the relative minor to C). It contains nearly the same notes as its relative major. For instance, Am = A, C and E, which is the same as C6 (minus the 5th). C = C, E, and G, which is the same as Am7, minus the root.

The reverse works as well: *For any minor chord, substitute its relative major.* The relative major is a m3rd (3 frets) above the minor. Thus, for Em play G, for Dm play F.

Extend this rule to include direct substitutes. That is, for C you can substitute Am7 or Am9; for CM7 substitute Am6; for Bm7 substitute D6.

"TONICIZATION" OF A MINOR CHORD

When a minor chord occurs in a tune, play its dominant (the chord that is a 5th above it) as a passing chord. This *"tonicizes"* the minor chord; i. e. momentarily makes it a tonic chord and strengthens its position.

Given this 2-bar progression: C/// | Am///   play: C/// | Am E7 Am /

The *tonicizing* dominant may be a major, minor, or dominant seven-type chord.

DIMINISHED CHORD SUBSTITUTION

For a diminished chord, substitute any other diminished chord that contains the same notes. As you learned on page 8, C^o, $E\flat^o$, $G\flat^o$ and A^o all contain the same four notes and are different inversions of the same chord. These four diminished chords are therefore interchangeable. Likewise, $D^o = F^o = A\flat^o = B^o$; and $E^o = G^o = B\flat^o = D\flat^o$.

DOMINANT SEVENTH/DIMINISHED CHORD SUBSTITUTION

For a dominant $7\flat9$ chord, substitute a diminished chord a 5th higher. Example: for $C7\flat9$ play G^o. An analysis of the two chords' intervals shows that, except for the dominant 7th chord's root, the chords are identical. ($C7\flat9$ = C, E, G, B$\flat$, D$\flat$. G^o = G, B$\flat$, D$\flat$, E.)

Extend this idea with direct substitution to arrive at this broader concept: *For any dominant seventh chord, substitute a diminished chord a fifth higher.* Example: For E7 play B^o.

The reverse of the first rule is also valid, since it's based on the fact that the two chords in question contain the same notes: *For any diminished chord, substitute the dominant $7\flat9$ chord a fifth lower* (which is the same as a fourth higher). Example: for A^o play $D7\flat9$.

The reverse of the broader rule can be used with caution, as it only works on occasion: *For any diminished chord, substitute a dominant 7th chord a 5th lower.*

Remember that you can extend this rule by DIMINISHED CHORD SUBSTITUTION. Thus, for E7 you can not only substitute B^o, but also D^o, F^o and $A\flat^o$.

AUGMENTED CHORD SUBSTITUTION

For any augmented chord, substitute another augmented chord a third or a sharp fifth higher. As discussed on page 8, an augmented chord is made of ascending thirds, and any of its three notes may be considered the root; that is C+ = C, E and G♯. Therefore C+, E+ and G♯+ are interchangeable. Likewise, D+ = F♯+ = A♯+... and C♯+ = F+ = A+.

FLAT FIVE SUBSTITUTION

For any dominant 7♭5 chord, substitute the dominant 7♭5 chord that is a flat fifth higher. The two chords contain identical notes. For example, G7♭5 = G, B, D♭, F. Its logical substitute, D♭7♭5, is exactly the same.

By extending this rule with direct substitution it becomes: *For any chord, substitute a chord that is a flat fifth higher.* This idea is often applied to CYCLE–OF–FOURTHS–type progressions and TURNAROUNDS. (See below.) Thus, for this two-bar phrase: G / Em /│Am / D7 / play: G / B♭M7 /│Am / A♭7♭5 /. B♭M7 is substituted for Em, A♭7♭5 for D7.

Flat five substitutes are often used as passing chords. For example, the two-bar phrase above can be played: G / Em B♭7 │ Am E♭9 D9 A♭7♭5. B♭7 is a flat five substitute for Em; it's also a passing chord between Em and Am, or an APPROACH CHORD (see below) to Am. E♭9, similarly, is a ♭5 substitute for Am and an APPROACH CHORD to D9. A♭7♭5 is a ♭5 substitute for D9 and an APPROACH CHORD to G, the tonic toward which this VI - II - V - I progression is heading.

A popular use of flat five substitution is seen in the alteration of this II - V - I phrase: Am7 - D9 - GM7 becomes Am11 - A♭7♭5 - GM7.

APPROACH CHORDS

Precede a chord with the chord that is a half-step (one fret) higher or lower. This especially applies during TURN-AROUNDS and CYCLE–OF–FOURTHS progressions. It's a useful concept for the *comping* (back-up) guitarist.

Here's an example: For the two-bar phrase mentioned above, G / Em /│Am / D7 / play: G F9 Em A♭m │ Am D♯7 D7 G♭7.

CYCLE OF FOURTHS SUBSTITUTION

To add movement or variety to a progression go up a third or sixth above the tonic and "cycle back" by fourths, i. e. play the III or VI chord and keep playing chords a IVth higher than the previous one until you reach the tonic. This creates a VI - II - V - I or III - VI - II - V - I progression.*

For example, replace two bars of G with this VI - II - V - I sequence: G / Em /│A9 / D9 / ; or this III - VI - II - V - I progression: Bm7 / E9 /│Am7 / D9 /

For this two-bar sequence: C / / /│G7 / / / substitute a VI - II - V - I passage: C / Am7 /│Dm7 / G7 / .

Often, as in the above examples, the cycle of fourths doesn't reach the tonic within the substitution bars. Your final chord is a V chord. This usually works out all right in the context of the tune.

*See the MUSIC THEORY APPENDIX for more explanation of the cycle-of-fourths.

TURNAROUNDS

To add variety to the end of a musical phrase do a one-or two-bars-long "turn around the cycle of fourths." This is one of pop music's oldest tricks.

For example, if a verse ends with two bars of G, substitute: G / E9 / | Am / D7 or Bm / E9 / | A7 / D9 /.

You can use APPROACH CHORDS and FLAT FIVE SUBSTITUTIONS to create an infinite variety of turnarounds. Reread those sections to find some variations of the G—E—A—D turnaround.

DOMINANT MINOR SUBSTITUTION

For any dominant seventh chord, substitute the minor chord that is a fifth higher. This is like "cycling back" one step on the cycle of fourths. e. g: For C7, play Gm7...or play Gm7 followed by C7.

The reverse is also true: *For any minor chord, substitute the dominant seventh chord that is a fifth lower* (i. e. a fourth higher). For example: in place of Bm7, play E9, or E9 followed by Bm7.

SUBDOMINANT/FLAT VII SUBSTITUTION

Substitute a ♭VII chord for a IV chord (subdominant). Usually in this usage the ♭VII chord is a dominant seventh type. It can be added to the existing progression, as well as substituted, e. g., for this chord sequence in G: G / C / | G / / / play G / C F9 | G / / /. Here, the F9 is the ♭VII chord that was added because of the appearance of C, the subdominant.

The IV–♭VII-I sequence is often added, for variety, at the end of a cycle-of-fourths progression. For instance, the II-V-I progression is often expanded to read: II-V-IVm-♭VII-I. In the key of C: Dm9 / / / | G13 / / / becomes Dm9 / G13 / | Fm9 / B♭13 / .

SCALEWISE SUBSTITUTION

For any chord, substitute a series of chords based on the scale of the tonic. For example, for two bars of C, substitute: C / Dm / | Em Dm C / . (The Dm and Em chords are the IInd and IIIrd in the C scale.)

Scalewise substitution is usually an ascent or descent on the tonic scale. The example above is both; the chords go I-II-III-II-I. The chord types (major, minor, etc.) assigned to the scale degrees can vary, but the most harmonic and commonly-used choices are listed in the chart below.

For this scale degree:	I	II	III	IV	V	VI	VII
use this chord type:	I	IIm	IIIm or I/III	IV	V or I/V	VIm or IV/VI or IIm/VI	VIIo,VIIø or V/ VII or IIIm/VII

Chords based on the *chromatic* steps (chords inbetween the major scale degrees) can be major, minor, dominant seventh, diminished or half-diminished, according to context, as the examples listed below will show.

Scalewise substitutions need not be in any particular order. Two bars of G might be played: G / Bm7 / | Am7 / G / or: G / Bm7 / | Am7 Bm7 G /.

Chromatic chords can be diminished, as in this scalewise sequence: G G♯o Am7 A♯o | Bm7 A♯o Am7 G

Chromatic chords can also be major, minor, dominant seventh or half-diminished, as in these examples (once again, these are two-bar G variations):

Bm7 B♭m7 Am7 A♭7 | G7 Am7 G /   D♭ø C Bm7 B♭ø | Am7 A♭7♭5 G /

Note that none of these examples but the last one go higher than the third degree of the G scale. The last variation goes: ♭V–IV–III–♭III–II–♭II–I.

Here are some two-bar G variations that use the inversions listed in the scalewise chart:

G / Am7 / | A♯o / G/B /   G/D / D♭ø / | C / G/B /
(I)   (IIm)   (♯II) (I/III)   (I/V) (♭Vø)   (IV) (I/III)

Scalewise "runs" often connect chords. For instance, in this three-bar phrase in the key of G: G / / / | C / / / | G / / / scalewise substitutions can connect the I and IV chords:

G Am7 A♯o G/B | C Bm7 Am7 A♭7 | G / / /

You'll see countless variations of scalewise substitutions in the chord solos that follow this chapter.

COUNTER–MELODIES

Use substitution chords that create a simple ascending or descending counter-melody that complements the tune you're playing. The famous James Bond Theme offers a classic example; while the melodic theme is played over a minor chord, direct substitutions of that minor chord add a counter-melody. You'll hear the latter when you play these chords:

The tune itself can be played on the 1st or 6th string while the Em substitutions provide a counter-melody. Here are some other chord sequences that contain counter-melodies. In each case, a tune could be played on higher strings than those which contain the counter-melody.

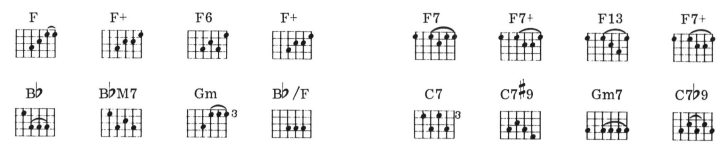

In the B♭ sequence, the Gm is a relative minor substitute. It's needed because it provides the G note in the B♭-A-G-F descending line. In the C7 sequence, Gm7 is a dominant minor substitute. It provides the D note in the counter-melody: E-D♯-D-D♭.

BASS LINE—DIRECTED SUBSTITUTION

Use chord substitutes that create an ascending or descending bass line; play a counter-melody in the bass. A scalewise substitution is one type of bass line-directed substitution. Here are some other types:

Hold a chord while changing its bass note; e.g. for two bars of C play:

The above can also be played this way, drawing substitutions from the scalewise substitution chart:

(I, IIIm/VII, VIm, I/V)

This popular minor progression, so useful as a counter-melodic substitution, can become a bass-directed substitution:

Cm - CmM7 - Cm7 - Cm6 becomes:

You can analyze the substitution choices by considering Cm the 6th degree of its relative major E♭ scale. Then the sequence becomes: VIm, V♯, I/V, V♭.

To sum up: A bass line-directed substitution can be a scalewise substitution (like a bass run with chords played for each bass note): it can be an ascending or descending bass line over a fixed triad; or it can be a bass counter-melody in which each ascending or descending bass note is the root of a chord chosen from the scalewise substitution chart. The chord solos that follow include many examples of each type.

COMMON TONE SUBSTITUTION

Substitute any chord that sounds appropriate and/or contains the desired melody note. This amounts to a re-statement of the *bottom-line substitution rule:* if it sounds o.k. it *is* o.k. Trust your ear.

It also implies that a substitution doesn't have to make sense or even have an identifiable name. "Outside" chords can be used to create dissonance, surprise or ambiguity. Elevenths, suspensions and chords like this one, made of ascending fourths: lend your music an outside sound.

****

All these substitution ideas are put to use in the twelve chord solos that follow. Each solo is heavily notated; every deviation from the basic chord progression is explained in terms of the "rules" in this chapter.

Play each solo and study the in-depth notes that follow it. You'll be comparing the original, simple progression to the jazzed-up version. Make sure you understand the particular use of each substitution method as it occurs in the tune.

SHENANDOAH

SHENANDOAH

Folk songs like this one have no written chord structure. They are handed down "by ear" and no two written versions are likely to be the same. Here's the basic progression on which this version is based:

C7 [F / / / | B♭ F / F7 | B♭ / / C7 | F / / / | B♭ / Am / | . Dm / B♭m / | F / B♭ / | Am / B♭ / |
F / / / | C7 / F /]

As you read the explanations below, compare this set of chords to the changes in the chord solo. The numbers in the explanatory notes refer to bars. The initial C7 chord is a "pick-up" chord that precedes the first bar.

PICK—UP) G♭7♭5 is a ♭5 substitute for C7.

1) The first three chords are a typical scalewise progression. So are the next three, which are the second and third degrees of the F scale, and lead to the IV chord that starts bar 2.

2) Cm7 is a dominant minor substitution for the F9 that follows. B7 is a ♭5 substitution for F9 and leads to B♭M7.

3) IV to V (B♭ to C7) is jazzed up with a scalewise (bass-directed) descending chord sequence based on the scale of the tonic F. Thus IV — V — I becomes IV — IIIm — IIm — V — I (B♭M7 — Am7 — Gm11 — C13 & C7+ — FM7). This is a common way to alter a IV — V — I progression. Try it in other keys.

4) The first four chords are a bass-directed progression: FM7 = I, Am7/E = IIIm/VII, E♭6 = ♭VII, D7 = VI. The latter is the only substitution that isn't drawn from the scalewise chart of "most likely choices." A° is a dominant 7th/diminished chord substitution for D7.

5 & 6) A long bass-directed descending sequence takes up both bars and contains typical scalewise chords. The run is a whole B♭ octave: B♭M7 = IV (to the tonic, F), III = a note (no chord), II = Gm7, I = n.c., VII = Em11, nearly identical to Eø, ♭VII = E♭13, VI = Dm11, V = n.c., ♭V = Bø, IV = B♭m6. The latter chord is minor in the original progression. E♭7 is its dominant minor substitute.

8) E♭9 is a subdominant/♭VII substitution for B♭M7.

9) This measure is a cycle of fourths sub for F: Am7, Dm7, Gm7 (and C9 of the tenth measure) are III, VI, II and V cycling back to I. D♭9 is a ♭5 sub for Gm7 and an approach chord to C9.

10) G♭7♭5 is a ♭5 substitution for C9.

(Measure 7 was not discussed since it only contains direct substitutions.)

AURA LEE

AURA LEE

Aura Lee is the folk melody on which Elvis' "Love Me Tender" is based. Here's the basic chord progression:

‖: G / / / | A7 / / / | D7 / / / | G / / / :‖ G / B7 / | Em / G7 / | C / Cm / | G / / / |

E7 / / / | A7 / / / | D7 / / / | G / / / ‖

1) Em7 is a relative minor sub* for G. It begins a bass-directed series of chords that continues into the next measure; the descending line is E, D♯, D♮, C♯. B/D♯ is a tonicization of Em.

2 & 3) A7sus — A7 — Am7 contains a counter-melody: D, D♭, C. The Am chords are dominant minor subs for D7. A♭7 is a ♭5 sub for D7.

4) A VI – II – V – I turnaround rounds out the four-bar phrase (of which this is the last bar). Em7 is VI, Am9 is II and A♭M7 is a ♭5 sub for V (D7). The GM7 of bar 5 is I. The tune's melody ends with the G6,9 chord, but the soloist creates an "ad-lib" melody to fill in the space that is left with the Am9 and A♭M7 chords.

5) Am6 and G/B are scalewise subs for G. They are IIm and I/III.

6) Em11 is a dominant minor sub for A7. All four chords of this bar, plus Am7 in the next bar, contain a descending counter-melody: F♯, E, D, C♯, C♮.

7) The Am chords are dominant minor subs for D7.

8) & 9) & 10) The last three chords of bar 8, plus the next two bars, contain a long chromatically ascending bass line: B, C, C♯, D, D♯, E, F. The passing chords of bar 8 are typical choices: I/III (G/B), IV (C), IV♯o (C♯o). The chords of bars 9 and 10 are direct subs for the given chords.

11) F9 and F7 are subdominant;/♭VII subs for C.

12) G, Am7 and B♭m7 are a scalewise progression; they are I, II, and II♯ leading to III (Bm7) in the next bar.

13) Bm7 is a dominant minor sub for E7. F9♭5 is a ♭5 sub for Bm7 (a sub for a sub) and an approach chord to E7.

14) The dominant seventh A chords plus the first chord of bar 15 contain a descending counter-melody: F♯, E, D, C♯, C♮.

15) A♭7♯9 is a ♭5 sub for D7.

16) Em7 is a relative minor sub for G. This bar plus the next contain a closing ad-lib counter melody: A, G, F♯, E, F♯.

*For the sake of space, "sub" will be used for "substitution."

FRANKIE AND JOHNNY

FRANKIE AND JOHNNY

Here's a bluesy treatment of this tune, including lots of turnarounds, cycles of fourths and scalewise progressions. The basic chords are:

```
|| C / G7 / | C / / / | / / G7 / | C / C7 / | F / / / | / / / / | / / / / | C / / / | G7 / / / |
| / / / / | C / / / | / / / / ||
```

2) C/E begins a scalewise descent from I/III to I. Dm7 = IIm, D♭7 = I♯.

3) C♯o is an approach chord to Dm7. Dm7 is a dominant minor sub for G7. The ♭9 in the bass of the G13 chord leads to Am7 in bar 4. Bar 3 can be considered a turnaround: C♯o is a sub for A (VI) because it's the same as Eo, the dominant/diminished sub for A. Dm7 is II, G13/A♭ is V.

4) Am7 is a relative minor sub for C. A♭m7 is a passing chord leading to Gm7, which is a dominant minor sub for C7. G♭7 is another passing (approach) chord, leading to F. The whole bar is a bass-directed run from VIm to IV (the bass line is: A, A♭, G, G♭, F).

5) C6/E is a C scalewise chord connecting FM7 (IV) to F's relative minor, Dm7. The three-chord run is: IV (FM7) — I/III — (C6/E) — IIm (Dm7).

6) Here we walk back up to F (IV) from Dm7 (IIm), this time using IIIm (Em7) instead of I/III.

7) F♯o is a passing chord connecting FM7 to Em7 (in the next bar). It could also have led back to C. Diminished chords can be used as passing chords to lead to many possible destinations.

8 - 10) Em7 begins a cycle of fourths that has been added to the given I — V— I progression of bars 8-10. Em7 = III; A♯7 is Em7's ♭5 sub and leads to A; A7 and Am11 = VI; A♭7♭5 is the ♭5 sub for D (II); G9 = V; F♯6 is an approach chord to G6 (I again).

10) The moving 3-note formation that motivates this bar is often used by blues players:

11) 12) and 13) The tune ends with a turnaround. A7+5♭9 = VI, D9 = II, C♯9 is a ♭5 sub for G (V), and C9 = I.

RED RIVER VALLEY

RED RIVER VALLEY

This arrangement is full of cycles of fourths and turnarounds.

D7 ‖ G / / / | D7 / / / | G / / / | / / / / | / / / / | / / / / | D7 / / / | / / / / | G / / / |

| G7 / / / | C / / / | / / / / | G / / / | D7 / / / | G / / / | / / / / ‖

The chord solo goes around the tune twice.

PICK-UP) Am11 is a dominant minor sub for D7. It expands the pick-up to a II − V − I turnaround.

1 & 2)   A cycle of fourths has been added to the I − V progression in these two bars: E7$\flat$9 = VI, Am9 = II, D7$\flat$9 = V, Gadd9 in the next bar = I.

3 & 4)   Em7 is a relative minor sub for G. The three chords that follow are a VI − II − V turnaround: B$\flat$7 is a $\flat$5 sub for Em (VI), Am11 = II, A$\flat$7$\flat$5 is a $\flat$5 sub for D (V).

5, 6, 7 & 8)   These bars contain yet another cycle of fourths: III − VI − II− V − I. Bm7 = III; F9$\flat$5 is a $\flat$5 sub for Bm, leading to E (VI); B$^{\circ}$ is a dominant 7/diminished sub for E; E7$\flat$9+ = VI; A13, A7+ and Am7 = II; D9 = V; A$^{\circ}$ is a dominant 7/diminished sub for D.

7)   The three A chords contain the counter melody: F$\sharp$, F, E, which continues to descend through the next few measures.

9)   Bm7 is a tonicization of the Em7 that follows in bar 10.

10)   Em7 is a relative minor sub for G. Dm7 is a dominant minor sub for G and D$\flat$7 is an approach chord to C (as well as a $\flat$5 sub for G).

11)   Am7 is a relative minor sub for C.

12)   Changing C to Cm and following it with F9 is a classic subdominant/$\flat$VII sub as described on page 12.

13 & 14)   Another cycle of fourths replaces the I − V − I progression. Bm7 = III; Em7 and E7$\flat$5 = VI; Am7 = II; E$\flat$9 is a $\flat$5 sub for Am; D13 = V; A$\flat$7$\flat$5 is a $\flat$5 sub for D.

15 & 16)   Yet another turnaround follows G6,9. It rounds out a 16 bar phrase. G$\sharp$$^{\circ}$ is the diminished sub for B$^{\circ}$, which is the dominant 7/diminished sub for E7 (VI); Am9 = II; D7 = V.

17 − 20)   D$\flat$$^{\varnothing}$ is a $\flat$5 sub for G, and it begins a bass-directed passage that descends from D$\flat$ and ends at Am7 in bar 20. The chords follow the "rules" of the scalewise chart: D$\flat$$^{\varnothing}$ = V; CmM7 = IV; Em11/B = III (Em is G's relative minor, so Em11/B replaces G/B); B$\flat$$^{\circ}$ = $\flat$III; Am7 = II. The Am becomes part of a II − V − I phrase leading back to G in bar 21.

21) Em7 is a relative minor sub for G.

22 & 23) Here's another cycle of fourths: III (Bm7) — VI (E+ and E7) — II (Am7) — V (D9) — a sub for I in bar 24.

24) The Cm7 and F dominant 7 chords are another subdominant/♭VII sub, as in bar 12.

25 & 26) The three chords starting with G are a bass-directed series; Bm7/F♯ = IIIm/VII; G/F = ♭VII. Dm7 is a dominant minor sub for G.

27) The Am chords are relative minor subs for C.

28) F9 is a subdominant/♭VII sub for C.

29 & 30) A VI — II — V cycle of fourths is combined with a descending bass line (G, F♯, E, E♭, D.) Em7 = VI; E♭7♯9+ is a ♭5 sub for A, the II chord; the D chords = V; and there's a ♭5 sub for D thrown in — A♭7♯9.

30) The first three chords of this bar contain the counter melody: E, F, F♯.

31 — 34) This series of chords, starting with a ♭5 sub for the tonic, is a much-used coda in which the ending note (G) is sustained while the chords descend chromatically, ending with the tonic. D♭∅ = ♭V; Cm7 = IV; B7♯9+ = III; B♭13 = ♭III; A7 = II; A♭M7 = ♭II; GM9 = I.

SWING LOW, SWEET CHARIOT

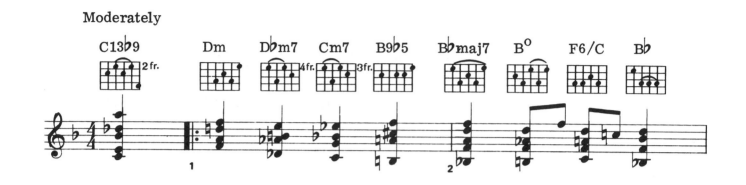

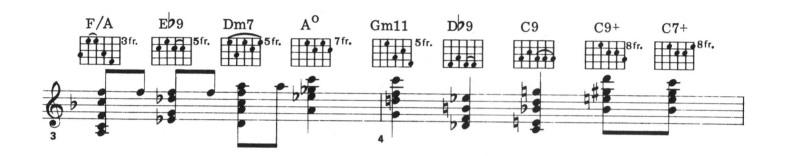

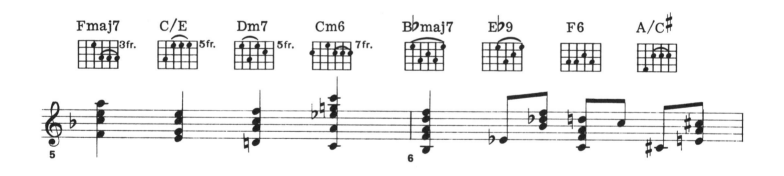

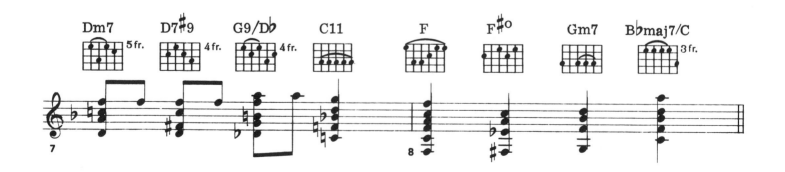

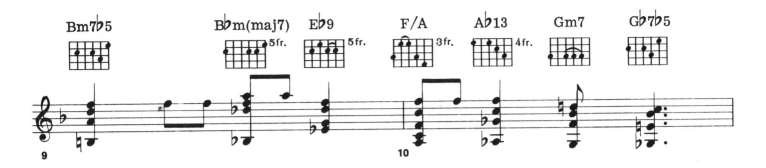

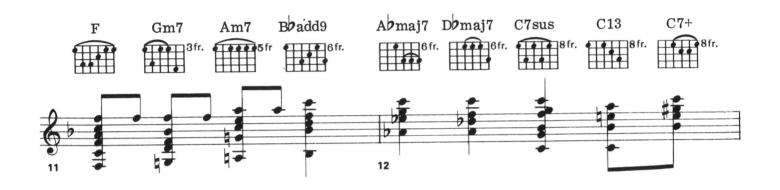

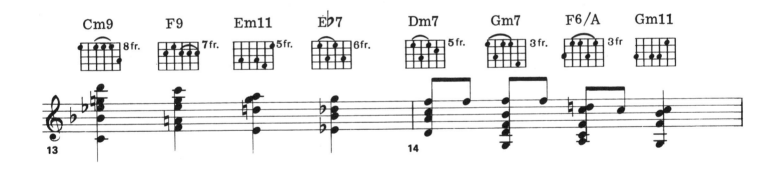

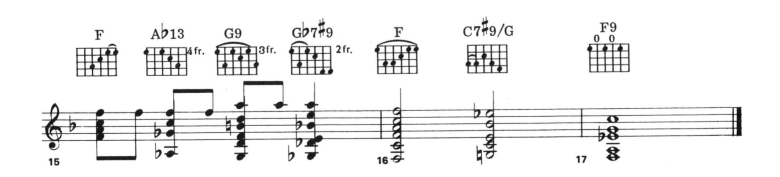

SWING LOW, SWEET CHARIOT

C ‖ F / F7 / | Bb / F / | / / Dm / | Gm / C7 / | F / F7 / | Bb / F / | Dm / G7 C | F / / / ‖

‖ F / / / | / / C7 / | F / Bb / | C7 / / / | F / F7 / | Bb / F / | F / G7 C | F / / / ‖

1 & 2)   Dm is a relative minor sub for F. These bars contain a moving bass line (Db, C, B, Bb, B, C). Dbm7 is an approach chord to Cm7, which is a dominant minor sub for F7. B9b5 is a b5 sub for F7.

2)   B⁰ is a passing chord leading from Bb to F. It's a dominant 7/diminished sub for Bb , since B⁰ = F⁰. This type of movement (IV, IV#⁰, I/V) is a common way to move from IV to I (or IV to I/V). Bb at the end of this bar, is a scalewise passing chord leading to F/A (I/III).

3)   Eb9 is an approach chord to Dm7. A⁰ is a dominant 7/diminished sub for D7 (which is never played). It *tonicizes* the Gm that follows.

4)   Db9 is a b5 sub for Gm.

5)   A descending bass line (F, E, D, C) leads to Bb in bar 6. Comparing the chords to those on the scalewise chart, FM7 = I; C/E = V/VII; Dm7 = VIm; Cm6 is a dominant minor sub for F7, or I/V. This is a typical scalewise movement from I to IV.

6)   Eb9 is a subdominant/ bVII sub for BbM7. A/C# *tonicizes* the Dm7 that follows. C#⁰ would also serve here as a passing chord from F to Dm.

7)   The G9 inversion (with the b5 in the bass) was chosen to create the descending bass line: D, Db , C.

8)   Here's the same turnaround (at the end of an 8-bar phrase) used in bars 15-16 in RED RIVER VALLEY: I, I#⁰, IIm, V7. BbM7/C is an extended C11; it's the V7 of the turnaround.

9 — 10)   Compare these bars to bars 17—20 of RED RIVER VALLEY. The same bass-directed device is used. Bø (a b5 sub for F) = bV; BbmM7 = IV; Eb9 is a dominant minor sub to Bbm and is an incidental chord, not part of this chromatic descent; F/A = I/III; Ab13 = II#; Gm7 = II; Gb7b5 = I# and it leads to F.

11)   Here's an ascending scalewise progression that goes from I to IV diatonically. II and III are minor chords, as usual.

12)   The modulation (key change) to Ab is a common tone sub. The change back to the key of F is typical: up a fourth (to DbM7) and down a half-step (to C). C13, C7+ and (in bar 13) Cm9 contain a counter-melody: A, Ab, G.

13 & 14)   Cm9 is a dominant minor sub for F. Em11 starts a cycle of fourths starting from VII: Em11 = VII; E♭7 is a ♭5 sub for A7 (III); Dm7 = VI; Gm7 = II; V is skipped entirely.

14) F6/A and Gm11 are III and II in a downward scalewise progression toward F.

15) In this cycle of fourths the ♭5 subs create a downward bass movement: (A♭, G, G♭, F). A♭13 is a ♭5 sub for D7 (VI); G9 = II; G♭7♯9 is a ♭5 sub for C7 (V); and F = I.

16 & 17)   The ending V — I tag uses voicings that lend a bluesy sound.

HOME ON THE RANGE

HOME ON THE RANGE

D7 ‖: G / / | G7 / / | C / / | Cm / / | G / / |¹· / / / | A7 / / | D7 / / :‖

²· | D7 / / | G / / | / / / ‖ D7 / / | / / / | G / / | / / / | / / / | A7 / / |

| D / / | / / / | G / / | G7 / / | C / / | Cm / / | G / / | D7 / / | G / / | / / ‖

PICK-UP) A♭7♭5 is a ♭5 sub for D7.

1 & 2)   Compare this bass-directed descending G to C chord series to the similar I — IV series in bars 5-6 of SWING LOW. In this case, Bm7 = IIIm/VII; Em7 = VI; Dm11 is a dominant minor sub for G7/D (I/V); D♭7 is an approach chord to CM7.

3 & 4)   Am7 is a relative minor sub for C and it's the third chord in a three-chord bass-directed descent (the bass notes are: C, B, A). F9 is a dominant minor sub for Cm.

5 & 6)   Bm7 is a *tonicization* of the relative minor (Em) that follows. You can also consider Bm7 - Em a cycle of fourths extension of the given II — V — I (A7 — D7 — G) progression. The Em — G+ — G — A13 sequence contains a descending counter melody: E, E♭, D, C♯.

7)   E♭9♭5 is a ♭5 sub for A7.

8)   A♭7♭5 is a ♭5 sub for D7.

9)   Bm7 plays the same role as in bar 1: it's a IIIm/VII chord in the G scale, leading down, in this case, to G/F.

10)   D♭9♭5 is a ♭5 sub for G7, leading to C.

11 & 12)   Here's a descending counter-melody, starting with the C chord: C, B, B♭, A.

13 & 14)   Bm7 is the first chord in a cycle of fourths: Bm7 = III; Em7 = VI; A13 = II; the D chords = V; G6,9 (in the next bar) = I.

15)   Cm6 is part of a quick turn around that goes: I — IVm — I. Another, similar turnaround is: I — IV —IVm — I.

18)   A° is a dominant 7/diminished sub for D9. F♯° is a diminished sub for A°.

21 & 22)   The Em chords are relative minors to G. Along with A7 they contain a descending counter-melody: E, E♭, D, D♭.

23)   FM7 is an unexpected common tone sub for D.

24) A♭7♭5 is a ♭5 sub for D7.

25 & 26)   Am7 And G6/B are the IInd and IIIrd degrees of a I − II − III scalewise progression. D♭9♭5 is a ♭5 sub for G.

27 & 28)   Dm7, D♯o and C/E are the IInd, ♯IInd and IIIrd degrees of a "C" scalewise progression. Note that this scalewise progression is based on some other chord than the tonic. The chord upon which it's based (C) is *tonicized.*

28) F9 is a dominant minor sub for Cm.

29 & 30)   Here's a cycle of fourths: Bm7 = III; Em11 = VI; A7 = II; D7 = V.

30) Here's a scalewise ascent from V (D7) to I. D7 = V; C/E = IV/VI; D/F♯ = V/VII; and there's a sub, in bar 31, for G (I).

31) E♭/G represents a common ending device called the *false cadence.* Before returning to the tonic from a V chord, the ♯V chord is played. It contains the tonic note (G, in this case) so it's a common tone sub.

BURY ME BENEATH THE WILLOW

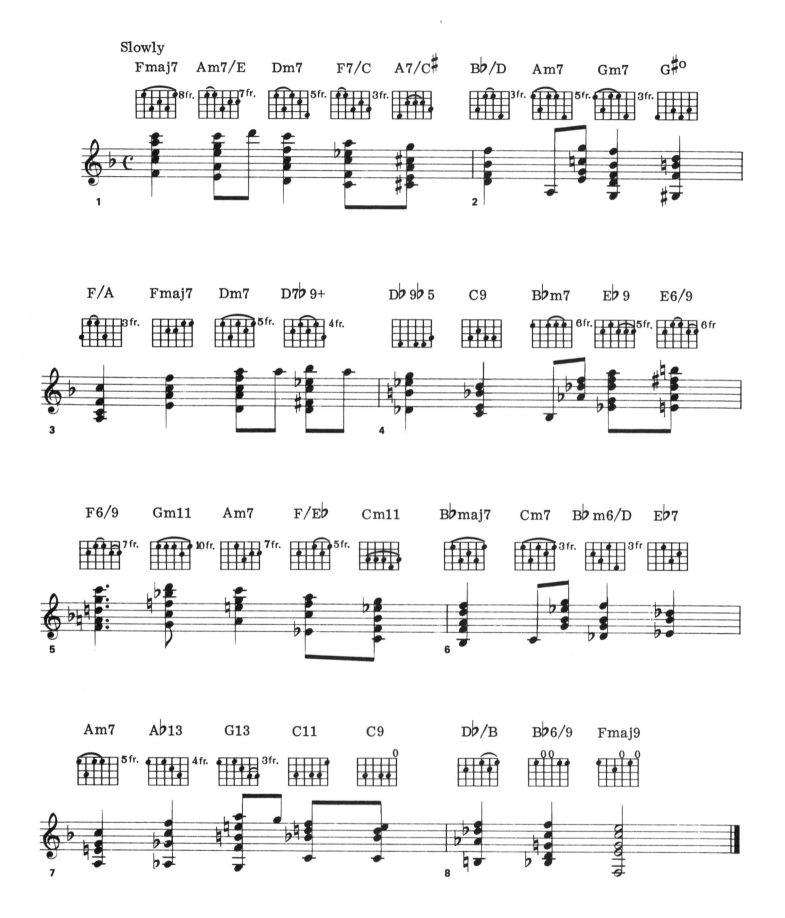

BURY ME BENEATH THE WILLOW

$\| F \ / \ F7 \ / \ | \ Bb \ / \ / \ / \ | \ F \ / \ / \ / \ | \ C7 \ / \ / \ / \ | \ F \ / \ F7 \ / \ | \ Bb \ / \ / \ / \ | \ F \ / \ C7 \ / \ | \ F \ / \ / \ / \ \|$

1) The first five chords are a bass-directed descent on the F scale that leads from I to IV (F to B♭). FM7 = I; Am7/E = IIIm/VII; Dm7 = VIm; F7/C = I/V; A7/C♯ is an approach chord to B♭/D. B♭/D (in the next bar) = IV.

2) Gm7 is a relative minor sub for B♭. Am7 is the passing chord in the F scale that connects B♭ to Gm7: B♭/D = IV; Am7 = IIIm; Gm7 = IIm. G♯°is a typical way of getting from Gm7 to F. The pattern is: IIm, II♯°, I/III.

3) & 4) Dm7 is F's relative minor sub. D7♭9+ sets up a cycle of fourths progression (where there was originally a V – I). D7♭9+ = VI; D♭9♭5 is the ♭5 sub for G (II); C9 = V; F6,9 (in the next bar) = I.

4) B♭m7 – E♭9 is a typical example of the subdominant/♭VII sub which expands a II – V – I into a II – V – IVm –♭VII – I. B♭m7 = IVm; E♭9 = ♭VII; E6,9 is an approach chord to F6,9 (I).

5) Gm11 and Am7 are IIm and IIIm in an F scalewise progression. Cm11 is a dominant minor sub for F7.

6) Cm7 is a scalewise sub for B♭. B♭m6/D♭ continues on up the scale. E♭7 is the subdominant/♭VII sub for B♭.

7) The given I – V – I progression is expanded to III – VI – II – V – I. Am7 is III; A♭13 is the ♭5 sub for D (VI); G13 is II; C11 and C9 = V.

8) D♭/B is D♭7 (with the 7th in the bass) and it functions here as a false cadence (see the end of HOME ON THE RANGE). D♭/B is a ♯V chord. But the B bass note sets up the B♭6,9 chord, giving us a IV - I (B♭ – F) ending.

LONDONDERRY AIR

Moderately

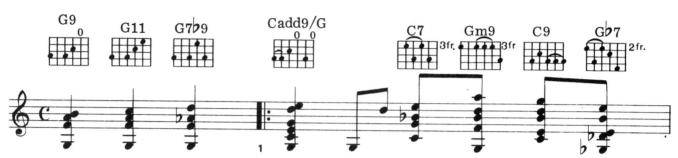

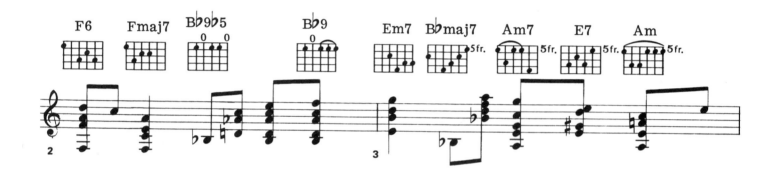

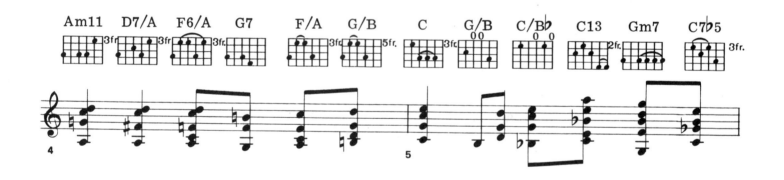

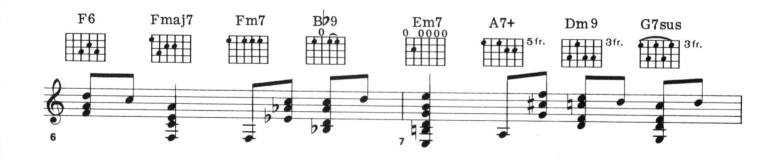

LONDONDERRY AIR

"Danny Boy" was based on this folk tune:

G7 ‖ C / C7 / | F / / / | C / / / | G7 / / / | C / C7 / | F / / / | C / G7 / | C / G / |

| C / G / | C / G / | C / Am / | G7 / / / | C7 / F / | Am / F / | C / F G | C / / / ‖

1) Gm9 is a dominant minor sub for C7. G♭7 is a ♭5 sub for C7.

2) The B♭ chords are subdominant/ ♭VII subs for F, leading back to the tonic, C. The first three chords of this bar hold the counter-melody: F, E, D.

3) & 4) The given I — V progression is expanded to a cycle of fourths. Em7 = III; B♭M7 is a ♭5 sub for Em7; Am7 = VI; E7 *tonicizes* Am; D7 = II; G7 = V. F6/A has a suspended sound, like F/G, since it's played where the ear expects a G (to complete the cycle of fourths).

4) The first three chords of this bar hold a counter-melody; G, G♭, F. The last three chords are a scalewise progression from V to I (G to C). G7 = V; F/A = IV/VI; G/B = V/VII; C (bar 5) = I.

5) The first three chords of this bar have a descending bass line: C, B, B♭. G/B is V/VII on the descending C scale. It's a passing chord leading to C/B♭, which is C7 with the 7th in the bass. Gm7 is a dominant minor sub for C7

6) Changing F to Fm7 and adding Fm's dominant minor sub, B♭9, is a form of subdominant/♭VII substitution. IV — I is expanded to IV — IVm —♭VII7 — I. Compare with bar 12 of RED RIVER VALLEY. Also the four chords of this bar contain a descending counter-melody: F, E, E♭, D.

7) A cycle of fourths is added to the given I — V — I. Em7 = III; A7+ = VI; Dm9 = II; G7sus = V.

8) The first three chords of this bar contain the descending bass line: F♯, F, E. F♯° is a ♭5 sub for C; Fm6 is a IVm chord, occurring typically at the end of an 8-bar phrase as part of a I — IVm — I turnaround. The *last* three chords of bar 8 are a diatonic scalewise walk up to VIm (Am) in the next bar. C/E = I/III; FM7 = IV; G7 = V.

9) Am7 is a relative minor sub for C. Em11 is a relative minor sub for G. Dm11 is a dominant minor sub for G. All these substitutes have expanded a V — I passage (G at the end of this bar and C at the beginning of the next) to read: IIIm — IIm — V — I.

10) C to G is expanded, by descending scalewise movement, to: CM9 (I); Em7 (III/VII); Am7 (VI); G (V).

10 & 11) G, in bar 10, begins a long descending bass-directed series with the bass line: G, F♯, F, E, D, C, B, A. Notice the "barber shop" sound of the first four chords in this series. They contain two contrary motions: while the bass line goes *down*, the chords go *up* the C scale. G = V; Am6 = IIm/VI; G/F = V/VII; C/E = I. The next three chords continue the bass line descent; they are a IIIm — IIm — I scalewise sub for C.

11) & 12) A cycle of fourths is added to the given changes: B° is a dominant 7/diminished sub for E7 (III); Am7 = VI; D9 and Dm7 = II; A♭7♭5 is a ♭5 sub for D; the three G chords = V; the cycle ends with C chords in bar 13.

12) The three G chords contain a descending counter-melody: E, E♭ , D. The C note in C7 (bar 13) carries it a step farther.

13) Dm7 is a relative minor sub for F. D♯° is a chromatic scalewise chord leading from Dm7 to Em7 (in the next bar). A° is a diminished chord sub for D♯°. All this would normally lead to the tonic, C/E.

14) Instead, it leads to Em7, which *tonicizes* Am7. B♭7♭5 is Em's ♭5 sub, and it leads to Am7. The B♭ chord also begins a descending bass line: B♭ , A, G, F♯, F, E. F♯° is a sub for Am7 (it's Am with the 6th in the bass). The given F (IV) chord is changed to IVm to effect a turnaround leading back to I.

15) Instead of I, we find a last turnaround (cycle of fourths). Em7 = III; Am7 = VI; E7♯9 tonicizes Am; B♭7♭5 is Am's ♭5 sub; A♭7♭5 is a ♭5 sub for D (II); G13 = V.

16) Still no I chord! G♯M7 — C♯M7 — CM7 (at last) is a false cadence, like the end of HOME ON THE RANGE. This, however, is a more complete version of the false cadence. It goes: ♯V (G♯M7) - up a fourth to ♯ I (C♯M7) — I (CM7).

AMAZING GRACE

AMAZING GRACE

The first time around this 16-bar sacred tune, the arrangement has a "gospel" flavor. The chord voicings and substitutions are in the style of black gospel music, that genre that has so influenced R & B and jazz. Gospel changes include lots of major triads and simple dominant seventh chords, diatonic scalewise progressions and chromatic diminished passing chords.

The second time around the arrangement has a more contemporary and outside sound. There are lots of suspensions, unexpected common tone substitutions, and ambiguous or borderline/dissonant changes, including nine-flat-fives, sharp nines and seventh-in-the-bass chords.

C7 ‖: F / / | F7 / / | B♭ / / | F / / | / / / | / / G7 | C7 / / | / / / :‖ G7 / C7 | F / / | / / / ‖

1 — 3)   These bars contain an F scale diatonic walk-down from I to IV: F = I; Am7/E = IIIm/VII; Dm7 = VI; Cm6 is a dominant minor sub for F7 (I/V); B♭ = IV. It's very similar to I — IV sequences in SWING LOW (bar 5) and HOME ON THE RANGE (bars 1-2).

3)   B° is a chromatic passing chord between B♭ (IV) and F/C (I/V). See SWING LOW, bar 2.

4)   C11 is a turnaround chord. It strengthens (re-tonicizes) the tonic F.

5 & 6)   Am7/E and Dm7 serve the same purpose as in bars 1-2, only here the walk-down stops at Dm. Notice that a cycle of fourths has been added: II — V (G7 — C7) has become: III (Am7/E) — VI (Dm7) — II (G7) — V (C7).

7 & 8)   C7 begins an F scalewise progression that goes from one C to another: C7 = V; B♭/D = IV/VI; E♭° = ♯VI; C/E = V/VII.

9)   C/E is the V/VII passing chord that leads to F's relative minor, Dm7, in bar 10. It serves the same purpose as Am7/E in bars 1 and 5 and is nearly the same chord (since Am7 is the relative minor of C).

10)   Dm7 is F's relative minor. A7 tonicizes Dm.

11)   B° serves the same purpose as in bar 3 — part of a IV — ♯IV° — I progression.

12 & 13)   F — FM7 — Dm contains the counter-melody: F, E, D. Dm is F's relative minor.

15)   This bar is a turnaround at the end of a 16-bar phrase. It's a scalewise progression: IV (B♭) — IIIm (Am7) — IIm (Gm7) — I (F, in the next bar).

16)   B♭9 is a pickup chord into bar 17, which starts the tune over. This voicing leads nicely to F6,9 since the two chords are so similar.

17) Dm11 is relative minor to F.

18) F/E♭ is F7 with the 7th in the bass. Cm11 is F7's dominant minor sub.

19) Making B♭ minor and following it with its dominant minor sub (E♭7) is a form of subdominant/ ♭VII substitution. Compare with bar 6 of LONDONDERRY AIR.

20 – 23)   The tonic is expected at the beginning of bar 20. A cycle of fourths has taken its place: Am7 = III; A♭13 is a ♭5 sub for D (VI); D7♯9 = VI; G13 = II; C7♯9 = V.

24) G♭9♭5 is a ♭5 sub for C7.

25 & 26)   Cm7 is a dominant minor sub for F7. The three 13th chords are common tone subs for F7. They each contain a melody note. Notice the interesting effect that is created by moving one formation down the fretboard.

26) B9♭5 is a ♭5 sub for F7. This 9♭5 formation resembles F+, so the E♭9♭5 that precedes it (same formation) is like an augmented sub.

28 – 31)   Bar 28 begins a long cycle of fourths progression. Am7 = III; Dm7 and D7♯9 = VI; G13 = II; C11 = V; F6,9 = I.

32 & 33)   B♭9 begins a IV – I final turnaround. E6,9 is an approach chord to F6,9♭5. The two chords are identical except for one note, so you slide up to the F chord. The F6,9♭5 closely resembles F+11. Plus eleven chords are often used as endings.

DIXIE

DIXIE

G7 ‖: C / / / | C7 / / / | F / / / | / / / / | C / / / | / / / / | G7 / / / | C / G /:‖

C / / / | F / / / | D7 / / / | G7 / / / | C / / / | F / / / | C / / / | G7 / / / |

‖: C / / / | G7 / / / | C / / / | G7 C / /:‖

PICK-UP) Dm11 is a dominant minor sub for G13.

1) C begins a scalewise descent towards Gm7 in bar 2. The same series could have led to C/G as well. C = I; C/B = VII (it's CM7 with M7 in the bass); Am7 = VI; A♭7+ is a chromatic approach chord to Gm7.

2) Gm7 is a dominant minor sub for C7. D♭9♭5 is a ♭5 sub for Gm7. G♭7 is a ♭5 sub for C9.

3) & 4) Dm7 is the relative minor to F. Em11 and A7, preceding it, are a "cycling back" on the cycle of fourths, or a *tonicization* of Dm7. D♯° is a passing chord that connects Dm to C. A° is a diminished sub for D♯°. This pattern (IIm − ♯II° − I or I/III) is a good way to get from IIm to the tonic. It resembles the IV − ♯IV° − I pattern in AMAZING GRACE bar 3 and SWING LOW bar 2.

5) & 6) C6, CM7 and Am7 have a descending bass line (C, B, A). Am7 is relative minor to C.

6)– 8) Am7 begins a cycle of fourths: Am7 = VI; E♭7 is Am's ♭5 sub; Dm11 = II; A♭7♭5 is Dm's ♭5 sub; G13 = V; C/E = I.

8) Dm11 is a dominant minor sub for G7.

9) & 10) Am7 is relative minor to C and it begins a descending bass line: A, A♭, G. The chords Am7, A♭7+ and CM7/G are the bass-directed equivalent of the minor series: Am, AmM7, Am7. (See Bass Line Directed Substitution, page 14, and compare.)

10) & 11) Em7/B starts a descending bass-directed diatonic C scale sequence leading from C to F (I to IV). Em7/B = IIIm/VII; Am7 = VIm; C7/G = I/V; FM7 = IV.

11) Gm9 is an F scalewise sub.

12) Here is a diatonic walk-up to IV from its relative minor sub, Dm7. Dm7 = IIm; Em7 = IIIm; F6 = IV. G7 sus adds the V chord to the scale. Though it's not in the given progression, it sets up the tonic.

14) E♭6 is a common tone sub and key change. A♭M7 is its IV chord and allows you to modulate back to the original key by dropping down a half-step to G. Compare this modulation to the one in SWING LOW, bar 14. Both tunes momentarily modulate up a minor third. It's an easy modulation to make (and to get out of) because the major scales of I and mIII share many of the same notes.

15) Dm11♭5 is a dominant minor sub for G.

16) Fadd9 is like a sus chord (F/G) in this context since it's followed by the "given chord" (G7) and has the same notes as G9 with a C note added.

17) — 19) Gb⌀ is a b5 sub for C, and it begins a long bass-directed descent similar to those in RED RIVER VAL-LEY (bars 17-20) and SWING LOW (bars 9-10). Gb⌀ = #IV; Fm6 = IV; C6/E = I/III; Eb° = #II°; Dm7 = II. Eb9b5 is a common tone sub and approach chord to D7, the given chord for this bar.

20) Ab9b5 is D7's b5 sub.

21) Am7 is relative minor to C. The preceding Em7 tonicizes Am7.

22) Dm7 is a relative minor sub for F and it starts a C scale bass-directed climb to IV (F): Dm7 = II; Em7 = III; FM7 = IV; F#° = #IV and it's an approach chord to C or C/G. See SWING LOW (bar 2) and AMAZING GRACE (bar 3) on the IV — #IV° — I/V sequence.

23) & 24) Instead of C, a cycle of fourths appears here: Em7 = III; Am7 = VI; Dm9 = II; Ab7b5 is Dm9's b5 sub; G13 = V.

25) Am chords in this bar are relative minor subs for C.

26) Ab7b5 is a b5 sub for the Dm or D7 that would normally appear between Am and G9 as part of a II — V — I sequence. It's an approach chord to G9+.

27) & 28) Em7 begins another cycle of fourths: Em7 = III; Am7 = VI; D9 = II; B° is a diminished chord sub for D°, which is a dominant 7/diminished sub for G (V): Am7 is the relative minor sub for C (I).

28) Bb7b5 is an approach chord to Am7, which is C's relative minor sub.

29) & 30) The Bb chord in bar 28 begins a series of bass-directed C-scale descending chords. Bb7b5 = bVII; Am7 = VI; Ab7+ = bVI; G7 = V; F#° = b5. Note that you can go many different places from a diminished chord. F#° could be followed by C. Instead:

31) & 32) Em begins another cycle of fourths. Em = III; Am7 = VI; Ab7 is a b5 sub for D (II); G9 = V; and, in bar 33:

33) Instead of C (I) Ab7 appears, as the start of a false cadence (Ab is a half-step above G, the V chord).

33) — 35) A typical way to end is to go up a fourth to Db and come down a half-step to C. This is *essentially* what happens here. The series of chords between Db and CM9/G are a Db scale bass descent: Db = I; Fm/C = IIIm/VII; Bbm7 = VI; DbM9/Ab = I/V. This final chord sets up the ending C chord. The Db descending scale chords contain a counter-melody that echoes the DIXIE melody (starting out just before Db: Eb, C, Ab, Ab, Ab, Bb, C, Eb, D). In other words, a counter-melody and simultaneous bass-directed descent are added to a false cadence.

BETTY AND DUPREE

Slow shuffle blues

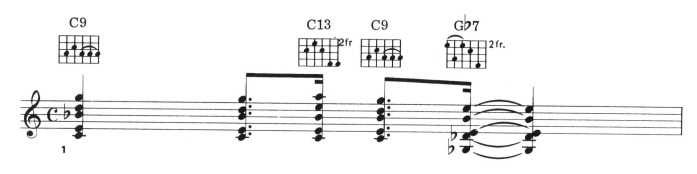

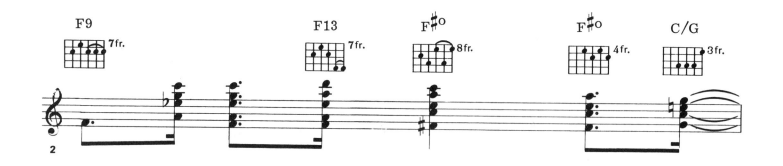

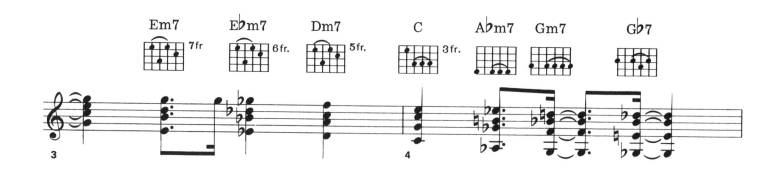

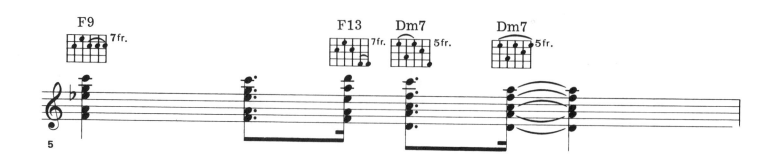

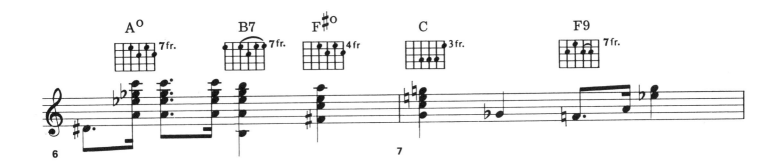

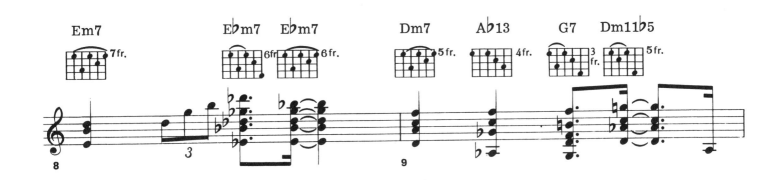

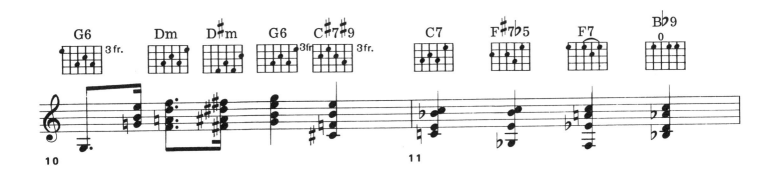

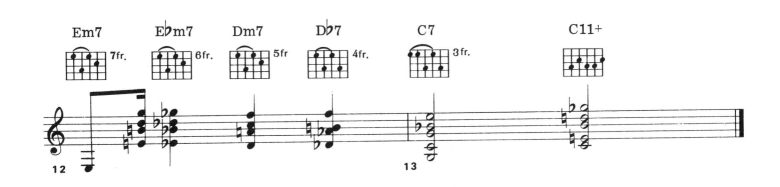

BETTY AND DUPREE

This arrangement shows how to jazz up a three-chord twelve-bar blues by adding cycles of fourths, scalewise progressions and jazzy voicings.

Like many blues tunes, BETTY AND DUPREE features two bars of melody followed by two bars of space, which can be filled by instrumental "answer-back" or ad-lib. This two-and-two-bar format is repeated three times (making a total of twelve bars). E.g:

C7 / //	F7 / / /	C7 / / / / / / /
BETTY TOLD DUPREE	I WANT A DIAMOND	RING (SPACE)

F7 / //	/ / / /	C7 / / / / / / /
BETTY TOLD DUPREE	I WANT A DIAMOND	RING (SPACE)

G7 / /	/ / / /	C7 / / / / / G7 /
DUPREE TOLD BETTY	I'D BUY YOU AN– Y	THING (SPACE)

1) G♭7 is a ♭5 sub for C7.

2) The F♯° chords are a scalewise transition between IV (F) and I/V (C/G). See SWING LOW, bar 2.

3) This bar is a scalewise descent to C (in the next bar): IIIm (Em7) — ♭IIIm (E♭m7) — IIm (Dm7) — I (C).

4) A♭m7 begins a scalewise descent to the F chord in bar 5. A♭m7 is an approach chord to Gm7, which is a dominant minor sub for C7. G♭7 is a ♭5 sub for C7 and an approach chord to F9.

5) The Dm chords are relative minor subs for F.

6) The diminished chords are subs for D♯°, which is part of a IIm — II♯° — I sequence (as in DIXIE, bar 4). B7, a fourth above F♯°, is a dominant 7/diminished substitute.

7 – 9) F9 is an approach chord to Em7, which begins a cycle of fourths: Em7 = III; the E♭m7 chords are ♭5 subs for A (VI); Dm7 = II; A♭13 is a ♭5 sub for Dm7; G7 = V; Dm11♭5 is G7's ♭5 sub; G6 is V.

10) Before we reach I (C), here is a whole bar of G and its subs. Dm — D♯m — G6 is a blues figure similar to that of bar 10, FRANKIE AND JOHNNIE. It plays upon the similarity between IIm and V9 (Dm and G9). C♯7♯9 is a ♭5 sub for G7.

11) We finally reach the C7 (I) at the end of the cycle of fourths (bars 7-10). Note that the cycle included a bass descent from F to D.

This bar features a I — IV — I turnaround. C7 = I; F$\sharp$7$\flat$5 is C7's $\flat$5 sub and an approach chord to F7 (IV). B$\flat$9 is the subdominant/ $\flat$VII sub so often used in this type of turnaround. Instead of it leading back to I we find, in bar 12:

12) A final turnaround: a cycle of fourths that features a bass run descending from E to C. Em7 = III; E$\flat$m7 is the $\flat$5 sub for A (VI); Dm7 = II; D$\flat$7 is the $\flat$5 sub for G (V); C7 is I.

THE OLD KENTUCKY HOME

THE OLD KENTUCKY HOME

This arrangement has a slightly more modern feel than the others. Many of the variations are common tone substitutions; that is, they are not easy to rationalize. Often, a particular chord formation is played in several different places on the fretboard to get two or three melody notes in a row. Lots of suspended, eleven, and six/nine chords are used to achieve an airy or spacey mood.

|1. _____ ||2.

C7 ‖: F / F7 / | Bb / F / | / / G7 / | C7 / / / :‖ / / C7 / | F / / / | F / Bb / | F / F7 / |

| Bb / / / | F / C7 / | F / F7 / | Bb / F / | / / C7 / | F / / / ‖

1) F6 begins a descending bass-directed progression: the bass notes are F, Eb, D, C. Dm7 and Dm11 are relative minor subs for F. Cm11 is a dominant minor sub for F7.

2) Gm7 is a relative minor sub for Bb. A6,9 is an approach chord to Bb6,9. Eb9 is an approach chord to Dm7 in the next bar.

3) Dm7 is relative minor to F. Bb13 is a common tone sub which has a *tonicizing* effect on Dm, since it's in Dm's chord family (Bb is the relative major to Gm). It also sets up Bø. Bø is the same as Dm with B (the sixth) in the bass; so Bø is a dominant minor sub for G13. G#13 is a common tone sub.

4) Eb/Db is a modulation to Eb, a m3rd above the expected C chord. To get back to F we move up a fourth to Ab M7 (when in doubt start playing a cycle of fourths); up another fourth to Db9; and drop a half-step to C11, which brings us back to F. D11 is a common tone sub.

5) But, not wanting things to sound too resolved, we never reach F. E11 is a common tone sub and it continues the moving 11th chords of bar 4. E11 has a *tonicizing* effect on Dm7 because it's followed by Eb7b5. (E11 — Eb7b5 — Dm7 resembles a II – V – I movement to Dm.) Dm7 is the relative minor sub for F. A13 is a common tone sub and an approach chord to Bb6.

6) A6 is an approach chord to Gm7. (A6 is nearly identical to its relative minor, F#m7, the more obvious approach chord to Gm7.) Gm7 is a relative minor sub for Bb. C13, the V chord, sets up FM7. Bø and Bb13 are a bass-directed walk-down to Am7 (in bar 7). Bø = #IV; Bb13 = IV; Am7 = IIIm.

7) & 8) Am7 begins a cycle of fourths: Am7 = III; the D7 chords = VI; G13 = II; Cm11b5 = V; C#7b5 is a #V — a false cadence which resolves the usual way: up a fourth to F#M7 and down a half-step to F6,9.

8) Bb M7/C is an extended C11 chord, a turnaround at the end of an 8-bar phrase. The Db chord that follows is a common tone sub; it's the same formation as the previous chord, raised three frets.

9) Dm11 is a relative minor sub for F. Gm7 is a relative minor sub for Bb.

10) & 11) Cm7 is a dominant minor sub for F7. It begins a bass-directed descent with the bass line: C, B, B♭, A, G. B9+ is a ♭5 sub for F7 and an approach chord to B♭. Am7 is a passing chord between B♭M7 and its relative minor sub, Gm7. This walk-down is within the C scale: B♭M7 = IV; Am7 = IIIm; Gm7 = IIm. G♯° is a C-scale chromatic chord that leads to Am7 in bar 12. It could also lead back to the tonic F or F/A.

12) This bar is a cycle of fourths. Am7 = III; A♭M7 is a ♭5 sub for D (VI); D♭M7 is a ♭5 sub for G (II); C7sus = V; FM7 in the next bar = I.

13) E♭9♭5 is a common tone sub which has the same notes as F7+. B9♭5 is a ♭5 sub for F which is also very similar to F+ (the top part of this chord is an augmented triad). E♭/D♭is a common tone sub for F7 and an approach chord to F/E♭(F with the seventh in the bass).

14) A6,9 is an approach chord to the following B♭ 6,9, as in bar 2. C13 sets up a return to the tonic, as in bar 6. Surprisingly, an Am7 follows, suggesting a cycle of fourths back to C will follow. The 13th chords that follow are unexpected common tone subs.

15) Am7 starts a cycle of fourths back to F. Am7 = III; E♭7 is Am's ♭5 sub; D7♯9+ = VI; D♭9♭5 is ♭5 sub for G (II); and the C chords = V. (Note the descending bass run: E♭, D, D♭, C.)

16) The ending bar has a false cadence. C♯/B = ♯V; F♯M7 is C♯'s IV chord; FM9 is a half-step down from F♯M7. Compare to the false cadence at the end of LONDONDERRY AIR.

COMPING

Comping is playing back-up chords to support a soloist. Comping guitarists often play a different chord on each beat of a 4/4 tune, drawing upon the same substitution ideas as a soloist. Here are some sample comping charts to practice. Play these and write some of your own.

BURY ME BENEATH THE WILLOW — F

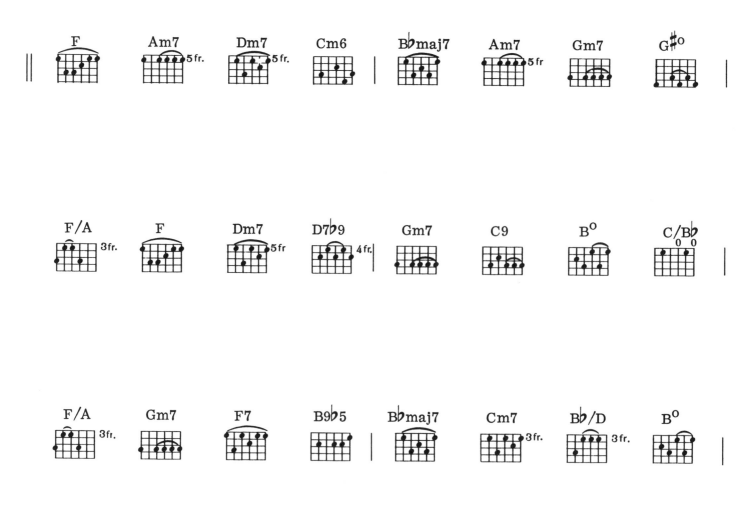

BETTY AND DUPREE — C

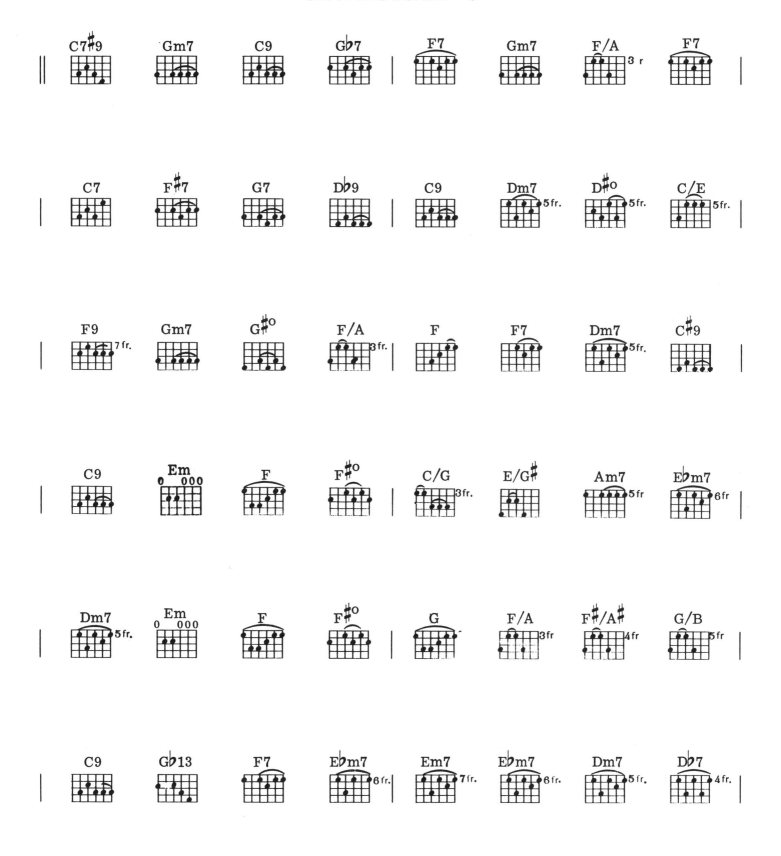

SWING LOW, SWEET CHARIOT — F

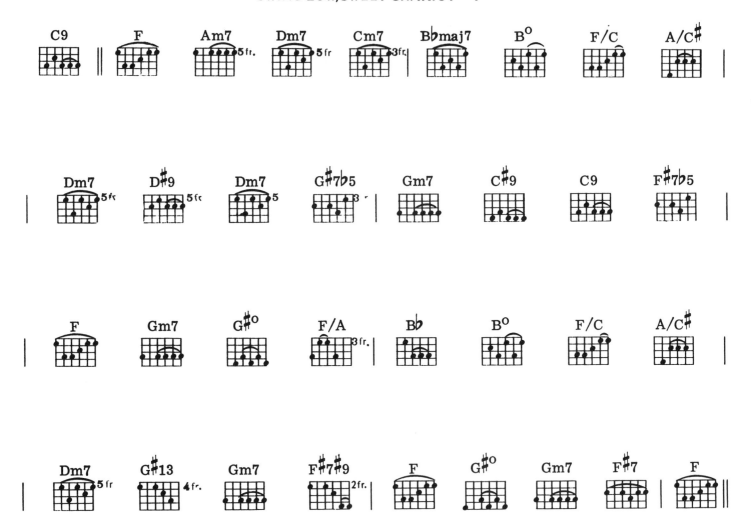

FRANKIE AND JOHNNIE – C

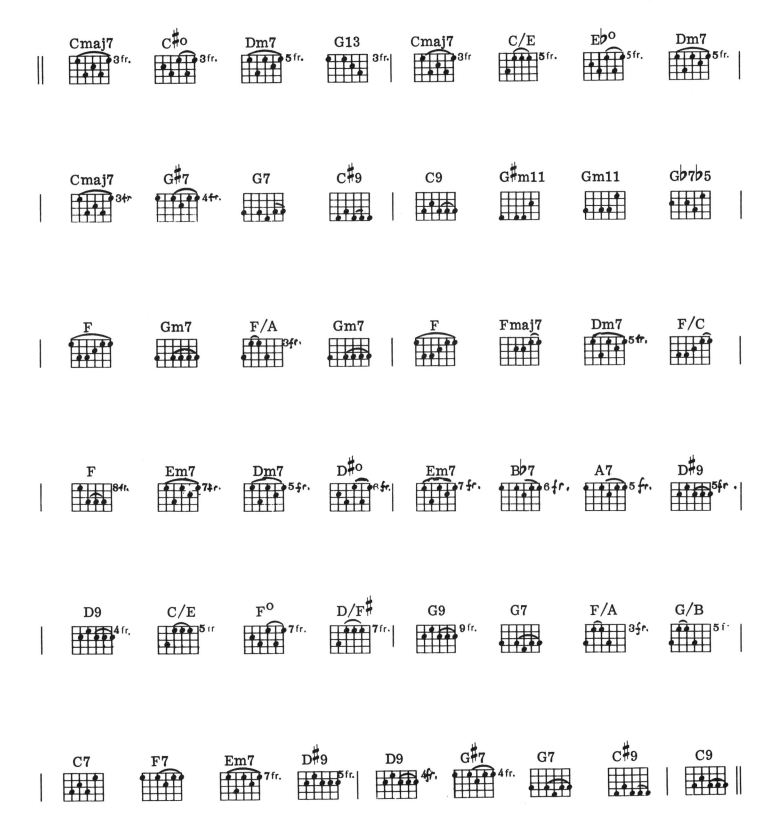

SHENANDOAH — F

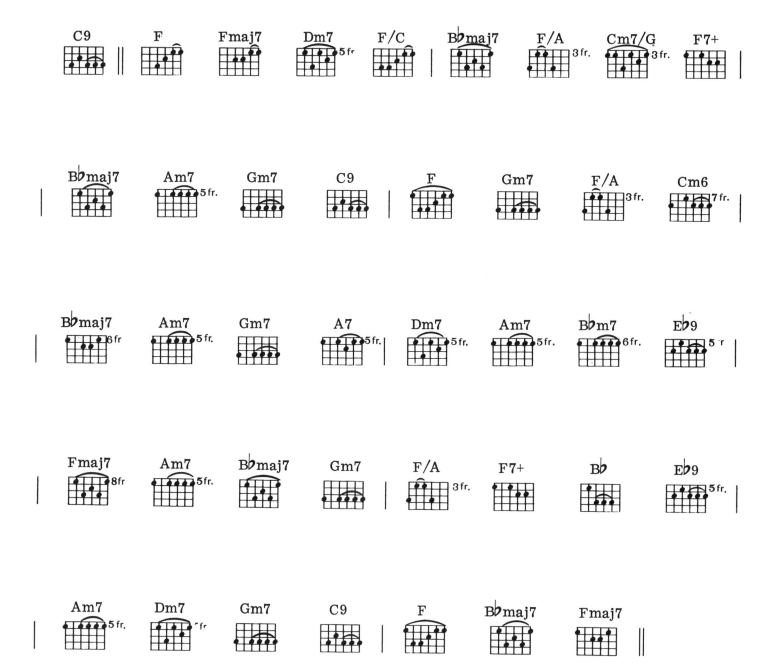

MUSIC THEORY APPENDIX

INTERVALS AND THE MAJOR SCALE

Intervals are fixed distances between notes. A *scale* is a certain number of notes separated by fixed intervals.

Here is a fretboard chart illustrating the intervals and notes that make up the *major scale.* This scale is composed of eight notes. The eighth note is the same letter-name as the first and is an "octave" higher. The example below shows an F scale.

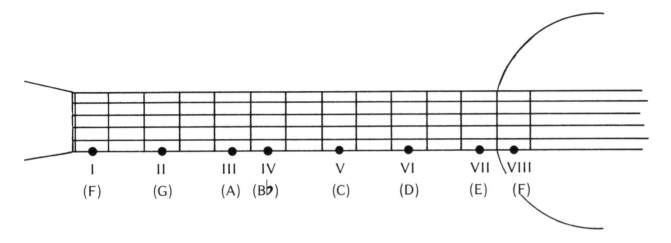

The distance of one fret on a guitar is a *half-step.* Two frets is a *whole step.*

The IInd note in the scale (G, in this case) is a whole step above the Ist. This interval (a whole step) is called a IInd. Thus G is a IInd above F, and A is a IInd above G.

The IIIrd in the major scale is two whole steps above the Ist. This interval is called a IIIrd. Thus A is a IIIrd above F, and D is a IIIrd above B♭. B♭ is a IIIrd below D.

The interval between I and IV is likewise called a IVth; the interval of I to V is a Vth, and so on. The notes of the major scale are mostly separated by whole steps. Only IIIrd — IVth and VIIth — VIIIth are half-steps.

Sometimes the notes between major scale intervals are referred to with the terms *sharp* (up a half-step) or *flat* or *minor* (down a half-step). For instance, the distance of three frets (e.g. F to A♭) is called a flat third, or a minor third. E♭, in the F scale, is a flat seventh. C♯, in the F scale, is a sharp fifth. The degrees of the major scale (i.e. the IIIrd, IVth, Vth, etc.) are called *diatonic* steps; inbetween notes are *chromatic* steps.

CHORDS AND THE CYCLE OF FOURTHS

A *chord* is a group of three or more notes of certain intervals played simultaneously in a cluster. For instance, a major chord is made of three notes: the Ist, IIIrd and Vth of the major scale by which the chord is named. Thus F major = F, A and C, the Ist, IIIrd and Vth of the F major scale.

The Ist of any chord is called its *root.* This note gives the chord its name.

Chords in a tune revolve around a tonal center called a *key*. A tune in the key of F, for instance, is likely to begin and end on an F chord. The chords and melody of the tune tend to be based on an F scale. The F chord is called the *tonic* (or I chord).

Chords within a tune are often referred to by their intervalic relationship to the tonic. For instance, in a tune that is in the key of F, the B♭ chord is called the IV chord (or the subdominant). C is called the V chord (or dom- inant). A is the III chord, and so on.

The chords that usually make up a simple tune are the I, IV and V chords and their *relative minors*. (The minor chord that is a flat third below a major chord is its relative minor. Thus, Dm is F's relative minor, and F is Dm's relative major.)

The circle below arranges all twelve notes in a particular order: Each letter represents a chord. Each major chord is next to its relative minor. One step clockwise of each chord is its IV chord. One step counter-clockwise of each chord is its V chord. (E.g. B♭ is one step clockwise of F. B♭ is F's IV chord. A is a step counter-clockwise of D. A is D's V chord.)

Thus each chord on the circle is grouped with its immediate "family" — its IV and V chords and the relative minors of I, IV and V.

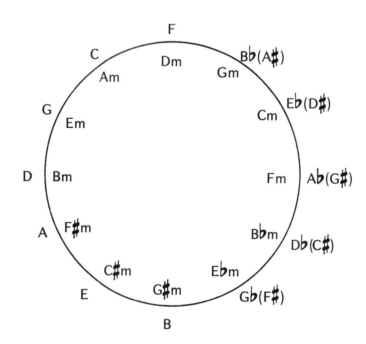

Many chord progressions move in a *cycle of fourths;* that is, they move toward the tonic by fourths. For instance, a common progression in F is: F – Dm – Gm–C7–F. Looking at the circle-picture, you can see that most of this chord sequence is simply clockwise motion on the circle; that is, after Dm you go up a fourth to Gm, up another fourth to C7, up another fourth to F, the tonic.

Some popular cycle of fourths progressions you should examine are (described by their intervalic chord relationships): II — V — I; VI — II — V — I; III — VI — II — V — I; VII — III — VI — II — V — I. Assign keys and letter names to these progressions and practice playing them. For instance, in the key of G, VI — II — V — I is: E — A — D — G. Change various chords to minors, sevenths, and so on, and hear how the progression sounds with these variations.

THE GUITAR FRETBOARD

In order to fully use the chord formation in the CHORD GROUP chapter, you need to know the notes on the guitar fretboard. Then you can make any formation correspond to a desired letter by matching its root note to the appropriate fret. Here is a fretboard chart that makes this possible by naming the notes on the fretboard.

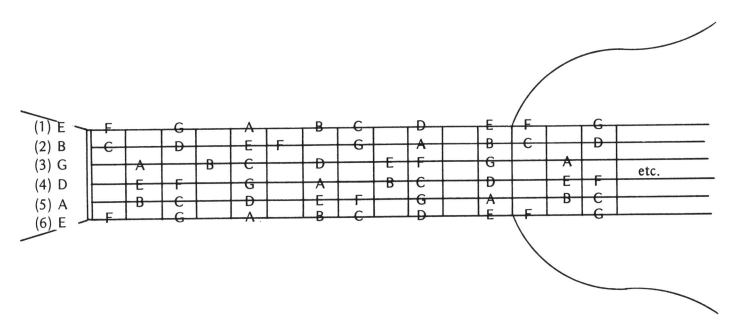

To find sharps and flats: G♭ is one fret above G; G♯ is one fret below G.

AFTERWORD

After studying these solos and all the substitution ideas, you have a lot of tools at your disposal for chordal jazz improvisation. The only way to master their use is to start using them.

Play any tune with which you're very familiar and work one substitution idea into it — such as cycling back by fourths or adding dominant seventh substitutions. And use that one idea to excess to find out when it does or doesn't work.

Play a tune in several different keys and/or different positions on the fretboard, because different chord formations suggest their own variations. Also, playing a tune in different keys helps you see it in terms of chordal intervals (IIm, ♭V, etc.) which is a much better way to visualize progressions than memorizing a set of changes in a certain key. To enhance your ability to understand progressions, analyze tunes (with and without your instrument at hand) in terms of intervals (e. g.: the bridge is four bars of G cycle of fourths, then it modulates up a minor third, etc.).

Above all, take chances. You can start an improvisational passage without knowing how it's going to resolve. Resolving it is half the fun. The best soloists sometimes find themselves out on a limb. The way they get back is what makes their solo exciting.

Also available from Schiff/Sokolow Publishing...

BASIC BLUES FOR GUITAR
by FRED SOKOLOW

The most thorough blues guitar book yet. Over 35 blues tunes cover electric and rock blues, folk, fingerpicking and bottleneck blues, B.B. King and Chuck Berry styles, jazzy blues and more. Plus positions, scales, chords, discographies and an overview of styles from Robert Johnson to George Benson.
Written in standard music notation and tablature with chord grids. All tunes are featured on the stereo CDbook.

BASIC ROCKABILLY FOR GUITAR
by FRED SOKOLOW

Learn the style that gave birth to rock'n'roll, with over 50 tunes, plus scales, fingering diagrams and licks. Explores the styles of rockabilly guitar pioneers such as Carl Perkins, Buddy Holly, James Burton and more.
Learn country blues, Travis-style fingerpicking, swamp rack, movable blues scales, chicken pickin', boogie bass lines, chord-based licks and other hot licks. Many backup and soloing styles are covered in tablature and standard music notation with chord grids.
Recording features all of the tunes and exercises - Lead and rhythm parts are separated in stereo.

For a free catalog with information on more Schiff/Sokolow Publishing and Fred Sokolow guitar and banjo books, recordings and videos write to:

Sokolow Music • P.O. Box 491264 • Los Angeles, CA 90049

sokolowmus@aol.com